Vibrations of my frequencies flow

Ronnie Cummings

BookLeaf Publishing

Presentation by *BookLeaf Publishing*

Web: www.bookleafpub.com

E-mail: info@bookleafpub.com

ISBN: 9789357440479

First edition 2023

My wife Amy

ACKNOWLEDGEMENT

Thanks to the Most High for blessing me with
the gift to be one of Her vessels!

PREFACE

This body of work gives the public a small
glimpse of my life as my pen writes.

Twenty-twenty-two

Fast how time flies:
seems as quick as 2022 came she was gone.
I was infatuated with her for 365 days.
The way she sounded off the tips of my lips
TWENTY-TWENTY-TWO…
It was something about her rhythmic vibration
that kept my frequency elated.

2022 I miss you,
But I'm glad you are gone.
She was convoluted with a large verity of
emotions:
Anger, regret, excitement, joy,
and love just to name a few
And I give thanks for all the lessons learned
From having her in my life for 8760 hours.
Thanks 2022 for all you brought me through…

Concrete Jungle

Traveling through the woods
Unable to tell the forest from the trees
Believing I'm not lost
When the reality is that I was blind
With my eyes wide open;
Thinking my moves were unbeatable,
Thought my drip could not, would not
Ever dry up,
Thought my pain could never end;
Lost, stuck in limbo
Continuing to Travel unfound
Experiencing life lessons
But missing the message
Until I reached the precipice
And just before I plummeted to my death,
The light bulb goes off and now I'm fighting
With all my might to stay alive,
Street surviving in this
Concrete Jungle…

Physically breathing

Hold me like hands hold gloves
Why do we fight the natural feeling of
Living in the moment? Is it the inevitable future
Or is it all an illusion designed to keep us
disillusioned,
stuck in futuristic confusion?

Why do we disagree with the person inside our
minds?

Maybe its insane for us to think the same or
perhaps its all a mental trap to keep us in chains,
boxes,
and frames like pictures that hang.
What's the rhyme or reason…IDK…
But I'm fighting to survive 'til I'm no longer
physically breathing…

K.R.S. O.N.E

(P.E.A.C.E) positive education activates creative elevation
In a nation where almost, everything is relative to
(F.E.A.R) false evidence appearing real.
In the only dimension that matters on this earthly plane.
However, most humans cannot handle the truth even if it
hit them in the face, so the first step is to unify and organize…
now that (S.L.A.P) sounds like a plan to
(S.O.S) save our souls from remaining
(S.O.S) stuck on stupid.
And all we have to do is
(K.I.S.S) keep it simple silly.
No huge elaborate rules (10 commandments)
Just two…
(E.M.I.L.Y) every moment I love you
And use the
(B.I.B.L.E) best instructions before leaving earth
As a guide because when we
(F.L.O.W) follow life's outcomes willingly
It becomes easy to know
(W.I.S.D.O.M) when I simply decide on more

We are reminded that the
(F.O.A.M.S) faith of a mustard seed
Is all that we need to
(F.A.I.T.H) focus and ignore these haters
Because
(F.A.I.T.H) for all it takes hope
To deal with
(S.T.R.U.G.G.L.E) you know those
Situations that remind us God's grace last
eternally;

When our young women of our communities
learn to
(L.A.D.Y) love and develop yourselves
Maybe then young men will begin to treat
women
As the Goddesses they are;

I had to quit the church once I
(R.E.L.I.G.I.O.U.S) realized every life in God's
image offers useful solutions.
Like
(D.I.E.T) did I eat that
Which has caused all these physical
complications…

But as long as we
(S.H.A.P.E) seek help and properly exercise
Unhealthy will not be our untimely demise…

So
(M.I.N.D) may I now direct
(P.O.W) poets of wackness
To the
(P.O.W) prisoners of war camps
For all these imposters
(M.I.A) missing in action
(L.O.L) laughing out loud
At all
(T.H.U.G) the hate you give
Because…
(K.R.S. O.N.E) knowledge reigns supreme over
nearly everything

Trunk of my tree

How much is enough to be fed up?
When will our lives become worth more than oil
and gold?
Because for 45 years I've only witnessed us
being treated less than burnt coal.

Where did our unity go?
What happened to the power of love?
As slaves we stayed,
As labors we raged at the imbalance of the
wage,
As colored we were murdered,
And as African/americans we ran,
but now I'm Black…
I Stand!!!

Why must our pain remain like bad stains in
your favorite jeans?
Is it the Negus blood flowing through our veins?
Or is it the Iron my chest is made of?

The Seed, taught me to grow in the snow,
The Root, dug deep to reach the truth,
The Bark, protects the flesh,
The Branches, connect to what's next,

And
The Leaves fall for more to one day evolve!!!

The Trunk of family Ancestry

Picture in a frame

9

Serious situations stressing sisters
Simultaneously struggling
To tactically trap transparent transgressions
That tragically traumatized teens
Approaching adulthood
Apparently accustomed to apprehension
Afraid of acting atrociously
In this nation's nuclear nonsense
Naturally nurturing numerous names
Attached to bodies and frames…
Sometimes words paint pictures clearer than
Those hung in frames…

Half a man

Half a man
Walking the land
Homelessly traveling
Life's lonely journey
Unafraid of death to come;
Living each day as if this may be it
That final step
That last breath;
Living in love
Following the Light's shine (signs)
As He divinely glides
Seeking only to enjoy
Laughter and Love
In a world lacking spiritual guidance
Caught up in senseless violence
Remaining silent allowing evil
To run rampant with no way to dampen
Mother's pain,
Regret,
And unrepentant shame
Living life in vain;
So to refrain from basking in sin
I dig deep within the depths of my essence.
And
Emerges God's shinning light
Forever illuminating the night...

Sleepless dreams

I woke up dreaming I was asleep,
Peacefully slumbering
While the sound of eight 'O' eights vibrated the
streets...

Wondering what could be so deep
To keep me comatose
while dope beats flowed melodiously through
the night's heat…

Watching myself
I slowly began to see signs of turbulence
As R.E.M began vibrating at a rapid
frequency…

Perspiration poured like water from an African
precipice…

Looking at my sleeping braw,
My facial features looked pissed and frowned…

But almost as quickly as the flood gates opened
they had suddenly disappeared…

My sweat dried up and

I instantly felt weird but clear…

I was returning to the fifth dimension and...

My subconscious woke aware…

Art of Poetry

Poetry comes in all shapes and sizes,
Costumes and disguises;
Literature flows like rivers and streams
Delegating historical fiction with uncut
restrictions
Picturing paintings described with poetical
phrases
That transform words into short stories
Which become novels and biographies;
Now extraordinary people present works
From women, men, and children
However pioneers of artistic poetical prose
Are often considered foes or heroes
By those whom come across primary sources
That expose the secrets of private diaries
Written in confidentiality
Only to manifest through the pen in journals,
Letters, and songs
To be sung all the years to come.
Historical events are often documented by
Poets, scribers, and historians in verse
Describing American Revolutions started
because
Of unproperly written constitutions
Preaching all are created equal

When our people were strung, hung,
And considered property in the
American system of slavery;
Civil war attempted to break the cycle
But it seems to only continually recycle
Like themes of P.E.A.C.E.
(positive education activating creative elevation)
Will always conflict with the struggle of war,
But once the discord ends
We finally realize what S.T.R.U.G.G.L.E. truly
is
(Situations that remind us God's grace last
eternally)

Savages...shall I continue

They call us savage…
Yet,
we were stolen,
Kidnapped,
Bought,
Sold,
And Taken from our homeland…
The Motherland…

Forced to walk through the door of no return…
which still stands today…

Yet, the oppressor calls us SAVAGE
God knows what happened on those long 3 to 6
months sailing trips…

But the facts are slavers didn't reach land with
the same amount of cargo
(humans, men, girls, and children) as they left
with…
Yet they call us SAVAGE…

So chained and shackled they (enslaved
Africans)
finally made it to shore

Where we were then stripped of our native
tongue,
Forced to cease and desist practicing our
religion,
And Forced to take new names…
Yet still, they call us SAVAGE…

Now some of the African Warriors never
stopped fighting…
Until death or
there was just no fight left in them…
If male, they would tie you down in front of
everyone
and have some other male take their manhood
(rape them)…

Yet they call us SAVAGE…
Once domesticated to their (slave owners) liking
we
Were then sold to the highest
bidder…considered property…

Yet they still call us SAVAGE…
They even performed experiments on us,
Breed us,
Interbreed us,
Made us sleep with our mothers,
(where do you think the term M-Fer comes
from)

But yet in some cultures they practice incest to
keep the blood royal so they say…

Yet again they call us SAVAGE…

Monticello was literally the 3rd president's of
the united states slave plantation
where he fathered numerous bastard slave
children…
FACTS…
But we are the SAVAGES…

SHALL I GO ON…

Fighting for my life all my life

  Running for freedom
        In the land of the free
And
        The home of the slave
        Not by choice
But
        By force.
        Using every ounce of adrenaline
        My body can muster.
        Legs begin to wobble
        Slowing down to a hobble
        Praying to God
        I don't trip, slip, or fall;
Prayers answered!
        Because just like that
        I found my 2nd breath
And
        Quickened my step
        Directly after giving thanks
        For the added strength
        Dispensed from the
Most High
        Guiding my strides,
        Blocking my scent

With fresh hard rain
Washing away
Generations of blood,
Sweat, and tragic pain
Sustained from the buyer's
Swinging whip;
Sprinting for my right to live my life as
peacefully as I like
But,
To acquire that I
Must fight for my life for all my life...

Tribal blood

When my mind clears
all fears disappear
into the abyss of lost nightmares
stuck in the conclaves of despair;

When my heart is pure
my wings begin to soar
into the atmosphere
unaware
of war declared to burst in air;

When my spirit is at peace
all physical,
emotional,
and psychological conflicts
cease to exist
in the presence
of the Light's essence;

When my pineal gland opens
all that is hidden becomes vividly in focus
like a sniper's one eye scoping
targets while floating;

When my flesh loses all of its' vitals

no more will I have foes or rivals,
just inform those that didn't know

Choctaw blood is why I was always so tribal…

WE ARE ALL FAMILY!

I'm 100% RACIST!

When I tell people this
I get a different reaction every time.

People's perceptions are so limited
that they only see what media,
government
and the other subliminal propaganda wants them
to see.

Me on the other hand,
I believe half of what I see
and very little of what I hear.

I know for a fact that I can procreate with any
female on planet earth.

And from that one fact
I conclude
that there is only one true Race,
the Human Race
and that is why I say

I am 100% RACIST

People in our world are so focused on gay
marriage,
bail being granted to serial killers,
face-booking,
and people switching genders
that we are losing our connection to the universe
and forgetting what truly matters…

…that we are all family…

God's hand in everything

As I gaze around at all these amazing God
created creatures
Averting my eyes would label me uncivilized;

From the bees that pollinate the trees
So that we can easily breathe,
to
The birds soaring gracefully through windless
skies.
Passing by watching with those hawk-like eyes
And everything too small for my visual to
optimize;

As I stare into the abyss of Earth's vast oceans,
Lakes,
Rivers and streams,
Mentally physically my body begins to stride
through
Salty H2O
Moving constantly
But not rapidly;

I'm to astonished to stop and wade in the water,
But moving slow enough to enjoy every living
moment

In the present
No need for technology's speed to snap pics
Of extremely exotic toxic swimming and flying
fish;

Then almost immediately I've transformed
From ocean to lake
Only recognized by the salt-less taste,
Fresh high quality drinkable H2O
Gracing my sophisticated palate,
Imaging fine dining at an inexpensive
5* dinner;
Admiring things I couldn't possibly have
dreamed
But mentally,
Physically
I can picture
God's hand in everything....

Prepared for the undeclared

My inner voice woke me this a.m.
by alarming my nervous system

that problems were on the horizon
in the form of viruses and bugs,
flus, and colds;

so I woke preparing for winter's storm;
struggling to gather strength because
my mechanical body is physically feeling sick,

ill like an opioid addict;
the crisis has begun
but decades ago crack
attacked like 11 safeties rushing the quarterback;

and no one cared to help or
assist with that;

so I start my day
prepared for the undeclared...

Induced

Induced to produce anti-toxic vapors
About government plotted capers
Makes it difficult to escape it…

Plans, plots,
and conspiracies

To make us disappear from history
Another long lost mystery;

Induced to produce prose written in verse
For choirs to recite in church
So religion can finally begin to do their job…

Because as many different religions as we have
today,
We would think we would live in Utopia,
But we live in organized chaos…

So what's wrong with us?

Some of us are induced to produce thoughts
That reduce and seduce instead of
Producing what's needed
For the next step of Evolution…

Love through

Now I've seen fire and I've seen pain
But Love is something I've yet to explain;

Like FOOTPRINTS IN SHADOWS
Love is hard to visually fathom;

With each NEW DAY
WILD FLOWERS
Sourround my SPACE with illustrious aromas
That WILL NOT FAIL
But will ALWAYS PREVAIL
At the Sun's FIRST LIGHT;

COLD DESPAIR
makes Love hard to declare;

WHEN NIGHT TIME CALLS
Moonlight grants Love a LEAP OF FAITH
That I HOPE TOMORROW
Will not erase;

BROKEN
hearts staring
FACE TO FACE
Remembering CLEAR AND NEAR

Without hope or fear
Praying your Loved one's picture never
disappears
From your DOOR'S OF ETERNAL LIGHT;

Now I've seen and felt earth's quake
And
Survived Her/Hurricane's stains,
But
Through ALLSEASONSVERSE
Deep inside my vibe
I know that no matter what

LOVE REMAINS OUR GUIDE…

Asphyxiation

Down in the drain,
Twirling round,
Gradually sinking,
Head spinning,
Body bending,
And heart trembling;

Aquatic perspiration from the circling
Anticipation of inevitable annihilation;

Like struggling in quicksand drowns you
quicker,
Pathological replies described as truth in
disguise,
Destroying the eternal chakra vibe...;

Switching the blame,
Weakening the master link of the chain,
Divided in spirit,
Lacking guidance and vision;

But continuing to reserve your right to battle
the never-ending deteriorating conditions;
Witnessing the demise of that glimmer
behind those eyes;

Watching the diminishing desire
to re-kindle a burnt-out flame;

Lacking the stick-to-it-tive-ness
to gather one's physical,
Mental,
And spiritual strength,
But too focused on other folks judgments;

Falling to the shadows,
Dwelling in the land of Babel where evil,
Death,
And pain are a constant around you;

Sinking down the drain,
Rotating like a caveman's wheel;

Dizzy is the feel;

Bloodshot plus blood-clots;

All of that circulation without proper ventilation
equals death by....

ASPHYXIATION!

Sound of silence

The sound of silence is golden
but listening to it is even better;

Silence reminds the quiet of the violence
suppressed in darkness
Trying to hide from being exposed in the light,
but the wicked flee when they feel the presence
of the Most High circling above like a halo
or wings that glow

while they glide in the night or daylight;

Witnesses call their sightings favor
while haters view the hue of the chosen as
blasphemous abuse

when they don't know who helped Hesus carry
the cross
(a heavy burden to tow)
Battered and bruised and the original hue
came true to assist the Sun
even though He was still illuminating the
masses!

The sound of what we can not hear

is as precious as the air we are favored to
breathe,

But most miss the gift we all are blessed to
receive everyday,

And most never give thanks for the breath that
we are blessed to breathe

And still refuse to acknowledge the Being that
created all of this!!!

Illuminating from within

The darkness consumes me like hunger to a
starving belly,
Surrounding every square inch of my thoughts,
Clouding my memories with delicious visions
of grander

Even though deep down I know it's just
ridiculous banter
Attempting artificial slander
Of a Bonafide name
Not searching for fame or fortune
But P.E.A.C.E and calm
However…

The darkness is relentless
Never giving up its quest
To successfully infiltrate my light
Waiting patiently for the lightest of a scratch
Or
A tiny little itty-bitty crack
To seep its gases into my essence's cerebral
cavity
To morph my mentality into insanity,

But my pupils keep me grounded…

Because my eyes are the windows to my soul
that allow God's shine to illuminate from my
bones

Black Glass Gorilla

All my life I've had to tread lite;

Walking on needles,
tipping and toeing,
Trying to remain unbroken,
Unscathed;
No blemish,

Because a single scratch
can immediately start a chain react

from a simple fracture,
a small crack can break
this Glass Gorilla's silver back;

Intelligence I possess it
but my presence is often rejected
because of my visual description;

clearer than water,
hard as diamonds,
yet still as fragile as spiderwebs;

I've always had to use adaptive reasoning
To avoid conflicts

Because just balling up my fist
When I'm pissed
Could end up catastrophically tragic,

So to enhance this Gorilla's lifespan,
I study what I am;

Created from heated sand,
Molded to stand grand
As an amorphous solid Black Glass Gorilla;
forever refracting God's light…

www.ingramcontent.com/pod-product-compliance
Lightning Source LLC
LaVergne TN
LVHW051239200726

843510LV00011B/1615